Discipline Over Distraction

Also by Stoic School

Atomic Stillness: The Small Daily Disciplines of a Stoic Life
Master Calm Through Stoicism
Discipline Over Distraction
The Stoic Habit: Mastering Your Mind in a Chaotic World

Table of Contents

Your Free Bonus: The 7-Day Overthinking Detox

Oftentimes, the best way to commit is to start a challenge. That's why I've created a 7-Day Overthinking Detox.

Each day, you'll get a small but powerful challenge—whether it's a mindset shift, a quick exercise, or a simple habit change—to start rewiring your brain away from overthinking and toward clarity.

Scan the QR code below to grab your free copy of this beautiful printable.

Introduction

Why You're Not Broken

What if the problem isn't you?

What if all this time, you haven't been lazy or unmotivated—but just **misled**?

In a world engineered to fracture your focus and hijack your attention, staying disciplined has become an act of rebellion. Every scroll, every ping, every advertisement whispering, "Just one more" — they're all competing for a piece of your mind. And more often than not, they win.

But it wasn't always this way. There was a time when people didn't need calendar hacks or dopamine detoxes to get through their day. A time when clarity, purpose, and calm weren't luxury items. That time wasn't just ancient history—it was **Stoic history**. And in those ancient teachings lies something profoundly modern: a solution not based on force or motivation, but on meaning and virtue.

This is a book about reclaiming your attention. About getting off the hamster wheel of modern distraction and into a life that's governed by your values—not your impulses. It's about remembering that discipline isn't about punishment or rigidity—it's about *alignment*. It's about creating a life where your actions reflect who you want to be. It's about self-respect.

Most self-help books try to fix you. This one assumes you're not broken.

DISCIPLINE OVER DISTRACTION

You're distracted, not disordered. Overwhelmed, not underpowered. And more than anything, you're likely misaligned—caught between the life you're living and the one your soul quietly longs for.

This book won't shout at you to "wake up at 5 AM" or give you a checklist of trendy productivity hacks. You've tried that already. It might've worked for a week or two, but then the noise crept back in. The fatigue. The frustration. The tiny voice whispering, "Why can't I just stay consistent?"

Here's the truth: consistency isn't built on hype. It's built on values. On self-trust. On rituals so rooted in who you are that *not* doing them would feel like self-betrayal. And that's where Stoicism comes in—not as a dusty philosophy from marble temples, but as a clear, modern toolkit for focus, calm, and character.

You'll meet Marcus Aurelius, the emperor who ruled an empire while journaling about how to rule himself. You'll hear from Seneca, who taught that time—not money—is your most precious resource. You'll walk alongside Epictetus, a once-enslaved man who proved that true freedom has nothing to do with your surroundings and everything to do with your choices.

But this isn't a history lesson. It's a manual. A guide. A mirror. You'll learn how to:

- Spot the invisible ways your attention is being stolen
- Rebuild the foundation of your habits from the inside out

- Make space in your life for stillness—without abandoning ambition
- Replace motivation with momentum and guilt with grace
- Choose structure over chaos without becoming rigid or robotic

In short, you'll learn how to build what the Stoics called your *inner citadel*—a mental fortress that protects your peace and directs your energy. From there, you'll move through distraction like a steady ship through stormy seas. You'll stop living at the mercy of the next notification or mood swing. You'll stop abandoning yourself.

So if you're tired of chasing clarity... if you're ready to stop consuming and start creating... if you crave a discipline that doesn't drain you but *frees* you—this book is for you.

Because in the end, the choice isn't between structure and freedom. It's between distraction and intention.

And one of those is slowly robbing you of your life.

Let's get it back.

Chapter 1: The War for Your Attention

"If you don't program your mind, someone else will."

— Zig Ziglar

I. The Hidden Enemy

You didn't sign up for this war, but you're in it.

Every time you check your phone and forget why. Every time your hand opens a new tab before your mind realizes what it's doing. Every time the day ends and you feel like you *did everything* but accomplished *nothing*. That's not a flaw in you. That's the battlefield.

The modern world is not just full of distractions—it is built on them. Entire industries thrive on your fractured focus. Your attention is the most valuable currency on earth, and almost everything around you is designed to take it from you.

Let's stop pretending that discipline is only about effort or grit. It's also about *defense*—about knowing that you are being targeted, nudged, tracked, and shaped in ways that make your old self-help goals feel naive. This isn't just about "focusing harder." It's about fighting smarter. Because what you're up against isn't just procrastination—it's an invisible machine engineered to keep you passive, addicted, and reactive.

It's time to expose that machine.

Not with paranoia, but with clarity. Not with fear, but with philosophy. Because once you see how this system works, you can finally break free of it. Not by escaping the world—but by becoming *stronger than it.*

II. The Economy of Distraction

There is a reason why companies spend millions crafting the perfect notification sound. It's not just cute design. It's manipulation. Every red badge on your screen, every autoplay reel, every infinite scroll feed—they were built with one goal: to override your will.

The average person checks their phone **96 times a day**. That's once every 10–12 minutes. Most people don't even realize they're doing it. Their thumb just flicks, their eyes just dart, and their mind is gone.

This isn't a moral failing. This is modern conditioning.

Our brains evolved for scarcity. We are drawn to novelty because, in the ancient world, novelty could mean survival. A sudden movement in the grass? That might be a predator. A new color on a tree? That might be fruit. We evolved to *notice*, not to *ignore*.

Today, that instinct is being exploited. You're no longer noticing real danger or opportunity—you're noticing memes, outrage, shiny headlines, seductive ads, and friend requests from people you haven't seen since primary school. But your brain doesn't know the difference. It just lights up.

And each time it lights up, **your attention resets**. You lose what researchers call "cognitive residue." That's the mental drag left behind when you switch tasks. When you bounce from deep work to a tweet, then back to your screen, you don't return where you left off. You return scattered.

Now do that 96 times a day.

The result? A society of people who are busy all day and deeply unfulfilled by night. People who *feel* exhausted, but can't name why. People who are surrounded by information, but starving for wisdom.

We don't have an information problem. We have an *attention* problem.

III. The Stoic View: You Become What You Give Attention To

This problem isn't new. Just louder.

Marcus Aurelius ruled the largest empire on earth and still wrote to himself in his journal, *"Ask yourself at every moment: is this necessary?"*

That was his version of closing tabs. He didn't have apps. He had generals. He had politics. He had plagues. He had grief. He had temptation and ego and legacy weighing on his shoulders. And yet, he recognized the fundamental truth that guides all of Stoic discipline:

Your attention is your life. What you focus on, you become.

Seneca called time "our most precious possession," and warned that most people give it away more easily than gold. He wrote about how men will protect their money, guard their property, and defend their reputation—but will let hours slip through their fingers without hesitation.

If that was true in ancient Rome, it is terrifyingly true now.

Today we trade our lives one swipe at a time. And unlike gold, we don't know how much time we have. Every distracted hour is an hour closer to the end. No refund. No restart.

The Stoics didn't fear death. They feared wasted life. And that's what makes their teachings so powerful in a distracted age—not because they lived without technology, but because they *trained themselves* to focus on what mattered even when the world tried to pull them away.

They called this inner clarity *ataraxia*—a kind of calm rooted in reason. A quiet mind immune to noise. That's what we need now more than ever.

Because while we can't stop the world from screaming, we can stop ourselves from listening.

IV. Training Yourself to See

The first skill of modern discipline is not action. It's awareness.

Before you can redirect your focus, you must first understand *where* it's currently going—and *why*. This is uncomfortable work. You may not like what you find. But clarity is the start of all control.

Spend a day tracking your attention. Not with an app. With your mind. Notice when you reach for your phone without thinking. Notice how often your tasks drift. Notice how many tabs are open, both on your browser and in your brain.

These tiny moments are not insignificant. They are the battlefield.

You don't need to judge yourself. You need to study yourself. The Stoics were always observing their impulses, questioning their emotions, interrogating their reactions. They didn't call it productivity. They called it philosophy.

Epictetus said: *"If you want to be free, then learn to see clearly. Begin with small things."*

That might mean putting your phone in another room while you write. It might mean delaying your response to a message. It might mean resisting the urge to post your thoughts immediately, just to feel seen.

Discipline begins here. In the pause.

Not with a plan, but with a pattern.

V. From Friction to Freedom

Most modern advice on focus tells you to download another app or rearrange your calendar. But that only works if the root of distraction is disorganization. It isn't.

Distraction is desire. And until you train your desires, you will always be drawn to the easy thing, the shiny thing, the noisy thing. That's not about tools. It's about self.

And yet, here lies the paradox: small acts of **friction** create large leaps in **freedom**.

Turning off your notifications is not about digital hygiene—it's about reclaiming your nervous system. Journaling for five minutes each morning is not about self-care—it's about programming your values into your day before the world does it for you. Choosing to read instead of scroll is not an aesthetic—it's a vote for the person you're becoming.

These small frictions—the ones that make your dopamine itch—are the path back to yourself. They're not always pleasant. But they are *liberating*.

The Stoics understood this. They practiced **voluntary discomfort** not to punish themselves, but to become less dependent on comfort. They knew that discipline wasn't a cage—it was armor. It let them move through life with intention instead of reaction.

And that's your opportunity now. Not to delete every app or live in the woods, but to move through the noise *without losing yourself in it*.

That's not rejection. It's refinement.

VI. The Attention Filter

What if, instead of trying to do everything, you filtered *everything* through one question?

Does this serve the person I want to become?

Not: Will this be fun?

Not: Will this get likes?

Not: Will this make me money?

But: Does this align with the life I'm trying to live?

This is the Stoic filter. It's not about being rigid or joyless—it's about being awake. It's about refusing to live on autopilot. It's about having a standard for your attention, and honoring it as sacred.

Imagine if you lived that way for a week. Imagine how much time you'd reclaim. How many mental loops you'd close. How much peace you'd find—not because the world got quieter, but because *you did*.

You can start that today. Not perfectly, but with intention.

Because the war for your attention isn't going to stop.

But you can stop surrendering.

What Comes Next

You've seen what you're up against. Now it's time to fortify your defenses. Not with willpower, but with *values*. Because until you know what truly matters to you, everything will matter too much.

In the next chapter, we'll explore how the Stoics built their code of virtue—and how you can build one too. Discipline, after all, isn't just about saying no. It's about knowing *what you're saying yes to.*

Let's build your foundation.

Chapter 2: The Stoic Code: Why Values Trump Willpower

"Waste no more time arguing what a good man should be. Be one."

— Marcus Aurelius

I. The Identity Shift

Some mornings, you wake up determined to change everything. You declare it's the day you'll finally stop scrolling, start meditating, go for a run, write that page, clean that inbox. You might even last a few hours. But then something small throws you off. A notification. A vague wave of boredom. A conversation that left a mark. Suddenly, the clarity is gone. The momentum fades. The cycle returns.

What happened?

Most people would say they lacked motivation. Or willpower. But that's not quite right.

You didn't fail because your will was weak. You failed because your identity was unclear.

When you don't know who you are—or who you're becoming—you will say yes to almost anything. That's because your internal compass has no direction. And without direction, discipline turns into a guessing game. Should you do this now or later? Is this a priority? Can you afford to skip this one thing? Without a deeper reference point, every moment becomes a debate. And as decision fatigue sets in, distraction wins.

That's why values matter more than willpower. Because when your actions are rooted in identity, there's less friction. There's less drama. You're not negotiating with yourself every hour. You're simply honoring your principles. Willpower fades. Values remain.

You don't need to become stricter. You need to become clearer.

This chapter is about building that clarity—the kind the Stoics called virtue. Not in a moralistic way, but in a directional way. As in: This is who I am. This is how I live. This is what matters to me, even when it's hard.

Once that foundation is set, discipline becomes less about effort and more about alignment.

II. The Stoic Blueprint: Virtue as Direction

The ancient Stoics didn't see virtue as some abstract ideal. They saw it as a practical guide for living. Virtue was the target you aimed at in every moment, the compass you used to navigate the chaos of the world. When everything else failed—fortune, health, reputation—virtue was what you could still control.

They defined four cardinal virtues: wisdom, courage, temperance, and justice.

These weren't vague concepts. They were tools.

Wisdom meant seeing clearly, choosing rationally, and making decisions based on what was true rather than what was popular or easy. It was about understanding the world as it is—not as you wish it to be—and responding with integrity.

Courage meant doing the right thing despite fear, fatigue, or risk. It wasn't about being fearless; it was about being willing to act anyway. Courage was the bridge between knowing what to do and actually doing it.

Temperance was self-mastery. Restraint. The ability to say no—not out of guilt or pressure, but because something higher mattered more. It meant choosing balance over excess, control over compulsion, stillness over chaos.

Justice meant fairness. Integrity. Living not just for yourself, but in a way that considered others. It was about responsibility, consistency, and making choices that didn't betray your conscience.

Together, these four virtues formed the Stoic code. They weren't commandments. They were commitments—to live by something deeper than impulse or external approval. To build a life that wasn't just efficient, but meaningful.

Most people today are chasing productivity, but they've lost sight of character. They want results without roots. And that's why their habits break down. Because motivation is a wave. But virtue? That's bedrock.

You don't need a to-do list. You need a compass.

III. From Values to Behavior

Imagine waking up tomorrow with no memory of your past habits, no routines, no lingering guilt about yesterday's failures. All you have is a blank slate and one question: What kind of person do I want to be today?

It's a powerful question. Because it resets the lens. Instead of asking, *What should I do?*, you start asking, *What would the person I want to become do?*

That's how identity-based discipline works. You're not just trying to "go to the gym." You're showing up as someone who values strength and consistency. You're not just writing a page. You're expressing the discipline of someone who respects their craft. You're not meditating because it's trendy. You're meditating because you value clarity and self-command.

This subtle shift changes everything. The task becomes an expression, not an obligation. You stop needing to force yourself into action. You just act, because anything else would feel out of character.

The Stoics practiced this daily. Marcus Aurelius constantly reminded himself who he was and what he stood for. He didn't wait for the world to reward him. He wrote in his journal, "Do not waste what remains of your life in speculating about others... Be straightforward and true."

This wasn't just personal reflection. It was self-programming.

And it's something you can do too.

You can define your values—not in some grand, performative way—but in a grounded, personal way. What matters to you? What are you unwilling to sacrifice? What kind of person would make you proud to look in the mirror?

Write those things down. One sentence per value. Not for the world. For yourself.

Then ask: How can I reflect this value today? Not in theory. In practice. In small, quiet acts.

That's the core of Stoic discipline: the integrity between your values and your behavior. Not perfection. Alignment.

IV. Building a Personal Code

A personal code isn't a list of rules. It's a short, living document that acts like an internal GPS. When temptation shows up, when you feel overwhelmed, when decisions blur—this code reminds you who you are and what you stand for.

You don't need many values. In fact, three is often enough. They just need to be real. Lived. Embodied. And they need to be visible in your actions.

For example, let's say your code includes:

Clarity

Courage

Consistency

Clarity might mean you begin your day with five minutes of silence or journaling—just to clear the fog. Courage might mean you confront that awkward conversation instead of avoiding it. Consistency might mean you show up to your creative work even when inspiration is absent.

It doesn't have to be perfect. It just has to be real. Because real builds trust. And self-trust is what discipline is ultimately made of.

If you break your word to others, they lose trust in you. But what happens when you keep breaking your word to yourself?

You stop believing in your ability to change.

That's why building discipline isn't just about tracking habits. It's about rebuilding integrity. Doing what you say you will do—not for applause, not for productivity, but for the simple dignity of being someone you can rely on.

That's what the Stoics did. And that's what you're learning to do now.

V. When Willpower Fails

Let's talk about what happens on the bad days. The low-energy days. The "I just don't care" days.

This is where most people give up. They think, If I can't show up perfectly, I've failed. And so they spiral. They skip a day, then a week. And suddenly they've abandoned the version of themselves they were building.

But that version doesn't disappear. It's still inside you—just waiting for you to stop outsourcing your identity to motivation.

Willpower isn't built for sustainability. It burns hot and fast. It's great for getting out of bed once. Not for showing up every day when you're tired, distracted, or discouraged.

Values, on the other hand, are resilient. They don't rely on mood. They don't care about energy. They just ask: What would it look like to honor my code in this moment?

That's why values always beat willpower.

You might not feel like doing the thing. But you do it anyway. Not out of force, but out of respect—for who you are, for who you're becoming.

And that's when something subtle shifts: your self-talk gets stronger. Your confidence returns. Not because everything's going well, but because you kept your word in the dark.

And those moments? They build real momentum.

VI. The Quiet Power of Identity-Based Discipline

The world celebrates explosive growth, loud hustle, and viral transformation. But real change is usually quieter. It's the person who says no to the thing that doesn't align. The one who builds rituals that don't need to be broadcast. The one who keeps showing up without waiting for permission.

That's what Stoic discipline looks like. It's not loud. It's anchored.

It's not about chasing intensity. It's about choosing integrity.

And over time, that integrity compounds. You become someone who doesn't need elaborate systems or endless hacks. You become someone who trusts themselves. Someone who knows: I might fall, but I will return. I might get distracted, but I will remember. I might be tired, but I will act in line with who I am.

That's the real secret. Not perfection. Not motivation. But alignment.

That's what makes discipline feel like freedom.

What Comes Next

Now that you've built the foundation—the code you live by—it's time to create the inner strength that protects it. Because values don't mean much if they crumble under pressure. And pressure is everywhere.

In the next chapter, we'll explore the Stoic concept of the inner citadel—your mental stronghold against chaos, distraction, and self-sabotage.

It's time to build the fortress.

Chapter 3: Building the Inner Citadel

"You have power over your mind — not outside events. Realize this, and you will find strength."

— Marcus Aurelius

I. The Fortress Within

There are moments in life when everything seems to shake.

A failed relationship. A health scare. A rejection letter. A sudden wave of anxiety that hits for no clear reason. In these moments, your environment betrays you. Your routines collapse. Your motivation vanishes. The structures you once depended on—job titles, daily habits, external validation—begin to fracture.

What's left?

This is the question the Stoics cared about more than almost anything. They weren't interested in fragile discipline—discipline that works when life is comfortable, and then disappears the moment pain enters the room. They were interested in resilience. In the unshakable kind of strength. The kind you can't see on the surface, but feel in someone's presence.

They called this resilience the *inner citadel.*

Imagine a fortress inside your mind—thick stone walls, silent corridors, a central chamber that no storm can reach. That's your citadel. And it's not built overnight. It's constructed slowly, decision by decision, value by value. Every time you choose calm over chaos, restraint over reactivity, clarity over confusion—you place another stone in that foundation.

The world will try to enter you through every open door. The citadel is where you learn to close them.

And in doing so, you stop depending on the world to stay grounded. You start depending on something far more reliable—yourself.

II. Control, Chaos, and the Stoic Divide

If we were to sum up Stoicism in one principle, it might be this: Know what is within your control, and accept what is not.

That sounds simple, even obvious. But most people live their lives doing the opposite.

They try to control what others think of them. They obsess over outcomes. They rehearse conversations that haven't happened and replay ones that already have. They try to predict the unpredictable and avoid the inevitable. In doing so, they exhaust themselves.

Meanwhile, they neglect the one domain they actually *can* control—their mind, their responses, their values, their decisions.

The inner citadel begins at the border between these two worlds: the world of control, and the world of chaos. When you confuse the two, you suffer. But when you learn to guard that border, you become powerful.

Epictetus put it bluntly: "There is only one way to happiness, and that is to cease worrying about things which are beyond the power of our will."

To stop worrying about what is beyond your will does not mean to become indifferent. It means to become *anchored*. It means to stop leaking energy into things you cannot influence and start reclaiming that energy to strengthen the part of you that always remains—your judgment, your effort, your character.

That's what lives in the citadel.

No one can take that from you. But you can forget it's there.

This chapter is about remembering.

III. Guarding the Gates

Your mind has entry points. Not literal doors, but open pathways—your attention, your emotions, your habits. Each one is a potential opening for the outside world to enter and rearrange your interior.

If you don't guard the gates, everything comes in.

The news. The noise. The opinions. The urgency of everyone else's lives. Over time, these inputs shape you. You become reactive. Restless. Easily triggered. Constantly shifting between identities depending on who's in the room or what's trending on your screen.

And eventually, you start to wonder why you feel so scattered, so disoriented, so unlike yourself.

It's because you haven't just lost focus—you've lost sovereignty.

That's why building the citadel requires awareness. You need to become the gatekeeper. Not paranoid. Not cynical. Just *discerning*. Not every thought deserves attention. Not every message deserves a reply. Not every urge deserves action. Not every invitation deserves a yes.

Start small. Begin by noticing what pulls you. What hijacks your peace? What triggers you, and why? What leaves you feeling uncentered?

These are signals.

They point to unguarded gates.

The Stoics were masters at this. When Marcus Aurelius journaled, he didn't just reflect—he filtered. He observed his mental habits the way a general inspects his soldiers. What am I allowing in? What am I reacting to? What am I making bigger than it actually is?

That level of inner management isn't obsessive. It's *liberating*.

It's the difference between living on defense and living with direction.

And the more you train this awareness, the more naturally you begin to return to center—even when life spins you off course.

IV. Practicing the Mental Rehearsal

A citadel doesn't just protect. It prepares.

DISCIPLINE OVER DISTRACTION

One of the most powerful Stoic exercises was called *premeditatio malorum*—the premeditation of evils. It sounds dramatic, but it's incredibly practical. The idea is simple: mentally rehearse what could go wrong, not to scare yourself, but to *strengthen* yourself.

What if this project fails?

What if the client walks away?

What if I'm misunderstood?

What if I lose the job, the relationship, the comfort I'm used to?

By imagining these scenarios—not obsessively, but intentionally—you begin to loosen your fear of them. You teach your mind that discomfort is not the end. That setbacks don't break you—they reveal you.

This kind of mental training isn't about pessimism. It's about realism. And more than that, it's about reclaiming your response.

Because when the thing actually happens—the rejection, the delay, the insult—you've already been there. You've already felt it, faced it, sat with it. So you don't panic. You pivot.

You've prepared—not for the worst, but for *anything*.

And that's when you realize something vital: most suffering comes not from what happens, but from being surprised by it. Shock turns discomfort into despair. Preparation turns discomfort into training.

That's why the Stoics practiced voluntary discomfort. They fasted, walked barefoot, slept on the floor—not to punish themselves, but to shrink the fear of those states. Once you've been hungry on purpose, hunger loses some of its bite. Once you've walked without luxury, you stop needing it.

And once you know you can endure more than you think, your mind begins to trust itself again.

That trust is the mortar of the citadel.

V. The Practice of Inner Return

No matter how disciplined you become, life will still throw you off balance. You will still get frustrated, distracted, discouraged. You will still feel lost some days.

That doesn't mean the citadel is broken. It means you've stepped outside it.

The goal isn't to live perfectly inside your fortress, untouched by life. The goal is to *remember* that the fortress exists—and to return to it more quickly each time you stray.

That's the practice. The return.

You lose your temper—then reflect and ask why. You waste a morning—then choose to be present again. You spiral into overthinking—then pause, breathe, and come back to what's within your control.

Each return builds strength.

And over time, you shorten the distance between reaction and reflection. You build what some call "recovery time"—the space between falling and regaining your footing.

This is real progress. Not just in discipline, but in peace.

Because peace is not a passive state. It's a *trained response.*

And the more you train it, the more natural it becomes. Until one day, you're standing in the middle of a stressful moment, and you don't flinch. You don't explode. You don't collapse.

You remain still.

Not because the situation isn't hard—but because *you've become harder to shake.*

That's the fruit of the citadel. Not perfection, but unshakable presence.

VI. Becoming the Architect

Most people spend their lives building external structures—resumes, titles, wealth, routines—and forget to build the only structure that matters when all else fails: themselves.

But the truth is, you are not just the occupant of your mind. You are the architect.

You get to decide what lives there. What principles shape it. What practices protect it. What kind of space it becomes for others.

And that's the final layer of the inner citadel—not just a private fortress, but a calm center that radiates outward.

When you've built this strength inside, others can feel it. Not because you preach it, but because you embody it. You become someone who isn't easily swayed. Someone who listens without reacting. Someone who moves with purpose instead of panic.

That doesn't just benefit you. It benefits everyone around you.

And that's the beauty of discipline. It starts as a tool for personal order. But done right, it becomes a gift to the world.

You carry stillness into rooms that have none. You carry clarity into conversations clouded by noise. You carry strength into spaces that are starving for it.

Not by controlling others.

But by mastering yourself.

What Comes Next

Now that the citadel is in place, we shift from protection to direction.

You've guarded your attention. You've built your code. You've fortified your mind. But now comes the true challenge: **focusing your energy on what truly matters**—not in theory, but in practice.

In the next chapter, we'll explore how to direct your firepower with intention. Not toward everything. Just one thing.

DISCIPLINE OVER DISTRACTION

It's time to master the Rule of One.

Chapter 4: The Rule of One: Mastering the Power of Single Focus

"You can do anything, but not everything."

— Greg McKeown

I. The Illusion of Progress

You've likely had days that looked full from the outside—tasks checked, emails replied, tabs open like soldiers in formation. You told yourself you were being productive. But by the end of the day, you felt strangely hollow. As if you'd been *busy* but not *effective*. As if your energy had been scattered across too many things, leaving you with nothing that truly moved forward.

This is the quiet trap of the modern world: the worship of activity without direction.

We confuse movement with momentum. We confuse effort with progress. And we applaud multitasking as if it were a skill instead of a liability.

At the center of all this confusion is a painful truth: we are afraid to commit. To one thing. One project. One habit. One path.

Why?

Because if you only pursue one thing, you can fail at it. You can be judged. You can disappoint yourself. But if you chase five things at once, you can tell yourself that at least you were "trying." You can stay safe behind the shield of divided attention.

But safety isn't freedom. And focus is not a constraint—it is power.

The Rule of One is the antidote to dilution. It's a discipline that cuts through the fog and demands clarity. It tells you: stop trying to do everything. Do one thing. Do it well. Do it now.

It sounds simple. But it's one of the hardest disciplines to live by—because it forces you to decide who you are, and what matters most.

And once you know that, the rest becomes noise.

II. The Cost of Fragmentation

The human mind was not designed for constant context switching.

Every time you jump from one task to another—from writing to messaging, from planning to scrolling—you leave behind a residue. Psychologists call it attention residue: the leftover thoughts, concerns, and mental loops from the previous task that follow you into the next. It's like trying to read a book while someone whispers in your ear about a completely different story.

This is why even a small distraction—just a glance at your phone—can disrupt your focus for several minutes. And if you multiply that by the dozens of micro-interruptions in an average day, it's no wonder deep work feels elusive.

We tell ourselves we're multitasking. What we're really doing is task-switching—and degrading our performance with every jump.

Research confirms this. A study from the University of California, Irvine found that it takes an average of 23 minutes and 15 seconds to return to deep focus after an interruption. Not seconds. Minutes. Which means those "quick checks" of your inbox or social feed are far more expensive than they appear.

And this isn't just about productivity. It's about *identity*.

When you're constantly switching, you forget who you are. You lose the through-line of your attention—the thread that ties your efforts to your purpose. You become fragmented. Drifting. Reactive. You begin to live at the surface of your life instead of moving through it with depth.

That's why mastering the Rule of One isn't just about doing more work. It's about becoming more whole.

It's about claiming back the thread.

III. The Power of Directed Energy

There's a reason a magnifying glass can start a fire—but only when it focuses light into a single point.

Your attention works the same way. Diffuse it, and it warms everything. Concentrate it, and it ignites.

The Stoics understood this long before the science. They weren't interested in chasing everything. They were interested in choosing wisely. Seneca once wrote, "To be everywhere is to be nowhere." A truth that echoes louder today than it ever has.

So what does it look like to live the Rule of One?

DISCIPLINE OVER DISTRACTION

It starts by identifying your *North Star*—the single intention, project, habit, or principle that you want to give your best energy to right now. Not forever. Just in this season.

Maybe it's writing a book. Maybe it's rebuilding your health. Maybe it's restoring a relationship, or developing a skill, or simply regaining clarity in your daily life.

Whatever it is, choose it fully. Let it become the lens through which you organize your days. Let it shape what you say yes to, and more importantly, what you say no to.

Because the Rule of One isn't just about addition—it's about subtraction. It's the discipline of removing distractions, obligations, and even good opportunities that do not align with your current priority.

That's the hard part.

Because you will feel the fear of missing out. You will feel the discomfort of turning down invitations, of slowing down, of not doing everything. But over time, you will feel something even deeper: a sense of direction. A quiet power. A clarity that others notice, even if they can't name it.

It's the calm confidence of someone who knows what they're about.

And that is rare.

IV. Making the Commitment

There's a reason the Rule of One isn't popular. It requires sacrifice.

You have to decide. You have to eliminate. You have to focus. And in a world that praises constant hustle and endless ambition, doing less—on purpose—feels rebellious.

But rebellion is what you need.

You need to rebel against the myth that more is always better. You need to rebel against the idea that your value is measured by how many tabs are open, how many roles you play, or how fast you respond.

The Rule of One begins when you ask: What truly matters right now?

Not what's urgent. Not what's trending. But what's *essential.*

Once you know that, you can begin to design your environment around it. Create space. Remove friction. Build rituals that protect your focus. You don't need 10 tools. You need fewer interruptions. You don't need perfect planning. You need consistent commitment.

Start with time blocks. Give your One Thing an hour of sacred time each morning, before the world makes its demands. Or guard your evening with intention, using it to reflect or build instead of scroll and numb.

Will you be perfect? No. Will you drift? Yes. But when you know your One Thing, you always have a compass. You can always return.

That return is the heart of the practice.

V. Living With Depth

The most beautiful part of the Rule of One is that it deepens your life.

You start to notice things you missed before. When you're not rushing from one task to another, you notice the quality of your breath. The tone in someone's voice. The feeling of stillness before you begin.

You stop multitasking through conversations and start listening with your full attention. You stop spreading your energy thin and start pouring it into something meaningful.

This depth creates richness. Not just in your work, but in your relationships. In your inner world. In your sense of time.

You no longer need every day to be exciting. You just need it to be aligned.

You don't need to achieve everything today. You just need to do what matters.

And ironically, the more you live by the Rule of One, the more you end up accomplishing. Not because you're doing more—but because your energy is no longer leaking.

It's being *channeled.*

That's the difference between motion and direction.

That's the difference between distraction and discipline.

VI. Trusting the Path

When you commit to one thing, doubt will follow. What if it's the wrong thing? What if you're missing something better?

That's normal. That's human. But the answer is not to keep switching. It's to keep going.

Because mastery is never found at the surface. It's found in the deep.

The Stoics knew this well. They were not concerned with novelty. They were concerned with wisdom. And wisdom doesn't come from chasing every option—it comes from standing still long enough to listen. To reflect. To understand.

The Rule of One teaches you to listen again. To focus your energy. To stay when it's boring. To commit when it's hard. To trust that the path is revealed through depth, not through speed.

You may not see results in the first week. You may not get applause for simplifying your life. But in time, you will feel the strength of it. The peace of it. The power of being rooted.

You will become someone who doesn't need constant stimulation to feel alive. Someone who doesn't chase ten dreams and catch none. Someone who moves through the day with quiet clarity, knowing exactly what matters and why.

That's what the Rule of One gives you. Not just focus. But direction. Not just output. But alignment. Not just discipline. But depth.

And in a distracted world, that's more than rare. It's revolutionary.

What Comes Next

Now that your focus has been reclaimed, your next task is to protect it—daily, deliberately, and with care.

In the next chapter, we'll explore how to make discipline automatic through rituals. Not rigid routines, but flexible structures that reinforce your values without draining your willpower.

Because focus is power. But *sustained* focus? That's freedom.

Let's build the system that makes that possible.

Chapter 5: The Ritual Reset: Make Discipline Automatic

"We are what we repeatedly do. Excellence, then, is not an act, but a habit."

— Will Durant, interpreting Aristotle

I. The Myth of Motivation

Every January, the world hits the reset button.

People declare fresh starts, new goals, grand promises. They sign up for classes, download habit trackers, rearrange their schedules. Motivation is high. The energy is real. Change feels possible.

But by February, the glow fades. Gym memberships go unused. Journals gather dust. The same people who were filled with hope now say things like, "I just lost momentum" or "I couldn't stay disciplined."

We blame ourselves. We say we lack willpower. We shame our inconsistency. But what we really lack isn't discipline. It's structure.

This is where the Stoics differed from today's motivational culture. They didn't rely on moods. They didn't wait for inspiration. They designed lives grounded in *ritual*—not as superstition, but as a form of spiritual and psychological scaffolding.

Marcus Aurelius didn't wake up every morning and "hope" to be Stoic. He reminded himself who he was, what the day might bring, and how he intended to respond. That was his ritual. A daily briefing for the soul. Seneca practiced evening reflections to review how he lived and what could be improved. Epictetus prescribed daily exercises in attention and restraint.

They didn't trust motivation. They trusted rhythm.

Because rhythm sustains what enthusiasm starts.

That's what we build here: not another list of habits to try, but a reset—a framework of rituals designed not to restrict your life, but to support it. Not to impress others, but to strengthen yourself.

This is how discipline becomes automatic: not through force, but through design.

II. What a Ritual Really Is

A ritual is not just a routine. It's a decision—made once, honored daily.

It's the difference between brushing your teeth because you "should," and brushing your teeth because it's part of who you are. No decision. No debate. Just rhythm.

Rituals provide structure without rigidity. They create containers in your day that hold space for your values to live. They reduce friction, automate behavior, and free up willpower for where it actually matters.

Think of them as lighthouses in the fog of your schedule—guiding you back to focus, intention, and clarity.

But most people misunderstand rituals. They think rituals are elaborate. Time-consuming. Reserved for monks or CEOs or morning-person influencers.

That's false.

A ritual can be five minutes long. It can be simple. Quiet. Personal. What matters isn't how impressive it looks. What matters is how consistently it aligns you with who you want to become.

If a ritual grounds you, it works. If it brings you back to attention, it counts.

And over time, these small acts of design become part of your identity. They become what you fall back on when life gets chaotic. What you return to when you lose your way.

Discipline doesn't disappear in difficult seasons—it hides inside your rituals, waiting to be reawakened.

III. The Power of Anchors

In Stoic thought, discipline was not about iron will. It was about *anchors*—daily touchpoints that pulled you back to reason, clarity, and virtue.

The Stoics knew the mind wandered. That emotions could overwhelm. That distraction was natural. But instead of trying to resist this, they prepared for it.

That's what rituals are: psychological anchors.

They remind you that you are not just a passenger in your day. You are the captain.

And a captain doesn't wait for calm waters to steer. They rely on instruments. Anchors. Routines that center them even in the storm.

A morning ritual might be as simple as journaling for five minutes. Not about feelings, but about framing the day: What will I face? How will I show up? What would a Stoic do?

An afternoon ritual might be a quiet break. A short walk. A chance to return to breath. To check in, recalibrate, reset.

An evening ritual might involve reflection. Not to judge yourself, but to observe. Where did I live in alignment? Where did I drift? What can I do better tomorrow?

These aren't productivity hacks. They're acts of self-ownership.

The kind that, over time, build an unshakable sense of self.

IV. Make It Easier to Succeed

The enemy of discipline isn't laziness. It's friction.

We often assume we lack discipline when we simply haven't made the behavior easy to start. If your guitar is in the closet, you won't play it. If your journal is buried in a drawer, you won't write in it. If your phone is the first thing you touch each morning, it will own your mind before your own thoughts get a chance.

Design matters.

Environment matters.

And most of the battle happens *before* the moment of choice.

That's why the best rituals are built on simplicity and proximity. Not effort, but ease.

You don't need ten-step systems. You need one clear step. One tiny start. One small win.

The Stoics didn't overwhelm themselves with morning perfection. They returned to the same ideas, over and over, because they knew the battle for the mind is daily. The repetition wasn't boring. It was training.

And so we reset the day before it begins. We clear the noise before it builds. We pre-decide who we are, so that when distractions arrive, they find a person who's already chosen.

This is how you make discipline easier: by lowering the cost of beginning.

By designing a life where the right thing is the *default*, not the exception.

V. When the Ritual Breaks

No matter how strong your rituals become, they will break. Life will disrupt them. Travel, illness, stress, family, unpredictability—they'll knock you off rhythm.

This is normal. What matters is how you respond.

The undisciplined mind turns a missed day into a missed week. It spirals. It says, "Well, I've already ruined the streak." It abandons the identity because the execution wasn't perfect.

But the disciplined mind does something very different. It *resets.*

Not with guilt. Not with shame. With clarity.

It returns to the ritual as quickly and gently as possible. It understands that rituals are not about streaks—they're about structure. The point isn't to never fall. The point is to fall *less dramatically*, and rise *more quickly*.

One missed day? Fine. Two? Reset. Three? Reflect.

This is how identity is protected. Not by perfection, but by return.

The Stoics knew this. Marcus Aurelius often chastised himself in his writings—not with anger, but with reminders. "You've wandered. Come back."

That is the Stoic path. The disciplined path.

Not flawless.

But faithful.

VI. Your Personal Reset System

You don't need to adopt anyone else's rituals. You need to build your own.

The ones that suit your life. Your energy. Your values. The ones that don't feel like tasks, but tools.

Maybe it starts with five minutes of silence before coffee. Maybe it's a moment of reading from *Meditations* before checking your phone. Maybe it's an end-of-day prompt scribbled into a notebook: "Did I act in line with who I want to be today?"

Simple. Personal. Repeatable.

Let it be imperfect. Let it evolve. But let it *exist*.

Because without it, you're vulnerable to the chaos of the world. You're dependent on how you feel, how much sleep you got, what mood you're in, whether the internet is being kind that day.

With it, you're grounded. Even when the world is loud.

This is the gift of ritual. It does not make you robotic. It makes you reliable.

And reliability is the cornerstone of trust—not just with others, but with yourself.

The more you return to your rituals, the more your mind trusts that you will show up. That you will guide it. That you are not here to drift—you are here to decide.

And when that trust is strong, discipline becomes automatic.

Not forced.

Chosen.

What Comes Next

DISCIPLINE OVER DISTRACTION

Your rituals are your reset. But what happens when emotions threaten to override everything? When anger, fear, anxiety, or overwhelm make you forget your own values?

That's where we go next.

Because discipline doesn't just live in actions—it lives in *emotion*. And mastering your emotions is not about suppression. It's about alchemy.

In the next chapter, we'll explore **emotional discipline**—the forgotten superpower that turns reactivity into resilience.

You've trained the body. Now let's train the mind.

Chapter 6: Emotional Discipline: The Forgotten Superpower

"No man is free who is not master of himself."

— Epictetus

I. The Quiet Saboteur

It's not always the environment that derails us. It's not always the distractions on our phones, or the clutter on our desks, or the noise outside our window.

Sometimes, the thing that knocks us off course is *inside* us—quietly, invisibly, emotionally.

A wave of anxiety that floods our focus. A flash of anger that pulls us into reaction. A cloud of shame that whispers, "You're not good enough." We don't always notice these moments until they've already taken control. And by the time we do, the day feels wasted, and we feel lost again.

This is why discipline can't just be physical. It can't just be about time blocks and habits and routines. It has to reach deeper—into our *emotional lives*. Because what derails most people isn't lack of strategy. It's being unprepared for the intensity of their own feelings.

This is what the Stoics understood better than most modern self-help philosophies. They knew that mastery of time, work, or behavior meant little if you were still a slave to anger, envy, fear, or pride. They believed true freedom came from emotional discipline—not as suppression, but as sovereignty.

They didn't reject emotion. They sought to understand it. To name it. To harness it. To prevent it from turning them into something they were not.

Because in the heat of emotion, it's easy to forget your values. It's easy to abandon your rituals. It's easy to speak, act, and decide from a place that you later regret.

Emotional discipline is the superpower that prevents that.

And like all superpowers, it's not given. It's trained.

II. The Modern Misunderstanding of Emotions

Our culture sends mixed messages about emotions.

On one hand, we're told to "listen to our feelings," to "follow our heart," to express everything or risk being repressed. On the other hand, we're mocked for being too emotional, too sensitive, too irrational. We're told to be strong, but not cold. Open, but not messy. Vulnerable, but always in control.

No wonder we're confused.

Stoicism offers a third path. A path of clarity, not confusion. It teaches us to *observe* emotions without being overwhelmed by them. To *respect* their presence, but not obey their every command. To treat them not as enemies or gods, but as messengers—worthy of attention, not submission.

This is not emotional suppression. The Stoics were not robots. They grieved, felt anger, loved, feared, doubted. Marcus Aurelius himself wrote about loneliness, irritation, despair. But instead of letting those emotions define him, he studied them. He stepped back from them. He reminded himself that the emotion is not the problem—it's what you *do with it* that matters.

The Stoic approach to emotion is about space. Creating enough distance between the stimulus and the response so that your values can speak louder than your impulses.

And that space—that tiny pause between feeling and action—is where discipline lives.

III. Anger: The Fire That Consumes

Let's begin with one of the most common—and misunderstood—emotions: anger.

Anger often feels powerful. It's quick. It's sharp. It gives the illusion of control. But most of the time, it's a trap. It narrows our thinking, hijacks our attention, and leaves destruction in its wake—words we didn't mean, actions we can't take back, a lingering sense of regret.

Seneca, in his essay *On Anger*, wrote that anger is "the most hideous and frenzied of all the emotions." He believed it was the one most likely to make people forget their humanity.

But he didn't say never feel it. He said, *question it*.

Is it just? Is it proportionate? Is it necessary? And most importantly: *Does it help?*

When anger arises, the Stoic path is not to deny it. It's to step back. To breathe. To recognize that the emotion is a natural flare—but you are not the flare. You are the observer. You get to choose what happens next.

Discipline in anger looks like silence. Stillness. A refusal to speak until you've cooled. It looks like writing instead of reacting. Like walking away instead of charging forward. Like waiting twenty minutes before you respond to that message that triggered something raw in you.

That's not weakness. That's wisdom.

And the more you practice this, the more your anger becomes a signal—not a leash.

IV. Anxiety and the Future That Doesn't Exist

If anger lives in the past, anxiety lives in the future.

It imagines what might happen. What could go wrong. It creates dozens of possible scenarios, most of which never arrive. And yet the body reacts as if they're already here. You sweat. You spin. You lose the moment you're actually living in because your mind has already left.

The Stoics understood this long before the term "anxiety" existed. They called it anticipatory grief—the pain of fearing something before it happens. Seneca wrote, "We suffer more in imagination than in reality."

And he was right.

Most of what we fear never comes. And when it does, we often handle it better than we expected. But that doesn't stop the mind from racing—unless we train it.

Emotional discipline with anxiety begins with returning to the present. The breath. The current action. It means asking, "What is in my control right now?" and doing *only* that.

Worry is endless. Action is grounding.

The Stoics didn't ignore danger. They faced it. But they refused to suffer *before* the suffering. They knew that fear exaggerates, while reason restores.

Your mind will try to escape the now. Pull it back. Every time you do, you place another brick in the foundation of your calm.

And over time, that foundation becomes stronger than the storm.

V. Envy, Shame, and the Comparison Trap

Envy and shame are two sides of the same distorted mirror. One says, "They're better than you." The other says, "You're not enough."

Both are born from comparison. Both are fed by a culture that tells you to measure your life by someone else's highlight reel. And both erode your ability to stay grounded in your own values.

Stoicism answers this with fierce clarity: *Stay in your own lane.*

Epictetus said, "If you want to improve, be content to be thought foolish and stupid." That sounds harsh, but it's liberating. It means letting go of needing to impress. Needing to compete. Needing to perform for a world that doesn't know your path.

Emotional discipline here means protecting your attention. It means limiting the inputs that trigger comparison. It means unfollowing what stirs insecurity. It means reconnecting to your own metrics for success—character, consistency, integrity.

You do not need to be better than anyone else. You only need to be in alignment with yourself.

Comparison is noise. Self-respect is signal.

Choose the signal.

VI. Mastery Through Reflection

You will feel emotions. You're supposed to. Discipline doesn't mean eliminating them—it means understanding them before they drive your actions.

The Stoics had a daily ritual to help with this: *evening reflection*.

Before bed, they asked themselves: Where was I triggered today? Did I act in line with my values? Where did I lose myself? Where did I return?

This wasn't punishment. It was alignment. A chance to learn. To improve. To train.

You can do the same.

One question. One sentence. One reflection each day is enough to begin strengthening the muscle of emotional awareness.

And awareness is the beginning of mastery.

You don't need to be emotionless. You need to be *self-aware*. From that place, you can channel emotion into something useful. You can turn anger into clarity. Fear into caution. Shame into humility. Pride into gratitude.

That's what emotional discipline gives you: not numbness, but *direction*.

You don't push feelings down. You rise above them—not to escape them, but to see them clearly.

And when you see clearly, you choose wisely.

That's the superpower.

What Comes Next

You've learned how to focus your energy. How to build structure. How to return to stillness. And now, how to stay grounded when your emotions surge.

But there's one final domain of mastery we haven't yet explored: how to remain *calm in motion*. How to keep your discipline *alive* even when life gets fast, noisy, and chaotic.

That's where we go next.

In the next chapter, we'll explore how to move through the modern world with stillness—how to live with urgency but without hurry, with ambition but without anxiety, with energy but without chaos.

Because true discipline isn't just about what happens in the quiet hours.

It's about who you are when the noise returns.

Let's finish strong.

Chapter 7: Stillness in Motion: Discipline in a Fast World

"It is not that we have a short time to live, but that we waste much of it."

— Seneca

I. A World That Doesn't Slow Down

Open your calendar. Look at your inbox. Look at the unread messages, the tabs open on your screen, the meetings booked back to back, the digital fragments of ten different tasks left half-finished.

Now, close your eyes for a moment and try to feel what your nervous system is experiencing.

Tension. Static. A slight pull in every direction.

This is the baseline for many of us. It's not that we've chosen chaos—it's that we've adapted to it. We live in a world that moves fast, demands more, and rarely gives permission to pause. Speed has become synonymous with success. Multitasking is praised. Urgency is rewarded. Rest is mistaken for laziness. And silence? That's something we fill, rather than feel.

But here's what no one tells you: if you live by the pace of the world, the world will always outrun you.

Discipline in a fast world requires a different kind of strength. Not to keep up. But to *slow down on purpose*. To remain still even as everything else accelerates. To say, "I will move at my own pace. I will not be ruled by noise. I will not measure my value in urgency."

That kind of discipline is rare. And it changes everything.

Because stillness in motion isn't passivity. It's power—quiet, controlled, intentional power.

It's how you stop being a passenger in your life and start becoming the one who steers.

II. Redefining Movement

Most people think of discipline as rigidity. Control. Tight schedules. Precision. But what if true discipline isn't found in inflexibility—but in *fluidity*?

Think of a martial artist. Their strength is not in tension, but in awareness. They flow, not because they're loose, but because they're grounded. They move with clarity because they know where their center is.

Stoicism teaches the same.

You don't need to freeze your life to live with intention. You need to move *with awareness*. To notice when your pace is being hijacked. To recognize when speed becomes panic, when ambition becomes burnout, when movement becomes escape.

Stillness in motion is the art of moving forward without spinning out. It's knowing when to act and when to pause. When to speak and when to wait. When to push and when to let go.

This is what separates the frantic from the focused. Both may be moving. But only one is rooted.

And that rooting begins with a decision: *I will no longer run from moment to moment unconsciously.*

I will bring myself back—even if the world doesn't.

III. The Space Between the Noise

It's easy to believe that you need more time.

More time to rest. More time to reflect. More time to get things in order. But what you really need isn't more hours. You need more space *within* the hours you already have.

That space isn't found. It's *created.*

A breath before the next call. A slow sip of water before you open your inbox. A moment of silence in the car before stepping into the chaos of home life. A pause between stimulus and response—just enough to ask yourself, "Is this who I want to be right now?"

This is how the Stoics found stillness.

Marcus Aurelius ruled over wars, pandemics, and betrayals—yet still found space in his day to write to himself. To return. To remember. Seneca urged us to "claim our time back," not by retiring to the mountains, but by mastering the present.

And that mastery happens in micro-moments.

One moment of intention can reset an entire day.

One breath of awareness can shift an entire response.

And these moments, added up, become a life of presence.

Not slower. Just *more yours*.

IV. The Paradox of Slowness

Here's a strange truth: slowing down makes you faster.

When you're intentional, you make fewer mistakes. You repeat yourself less. You recover quicker. You focus deeper. You finish what you start. And you waste less energy trying to remember what you were doing before distraction took over.

Slowness isn't a delay. It's an *investment* in clarity.

But the world won't clap for it. It will rush past you, offer a hundred things to chase. It will make you feel like you're falling behind for choosing depth over noise.

Ignore it.

Trust that your focus is doing something they can't see. Something foundational. Something rare.

When you move through the day with calm, it doesn't mean you're behind. It means you're no longer in a race you never agreed to run.

And when everyone else burns out trying to be everywhere, you'll be centered—fully present in the one place that matters: here.

That's the paradox.

Stillness isn't still. It's *efficient*.

It's quiet, but powerful.

Unimpressive to the world. Invaluable to your soul.

V. Designing a Slower Life in a Faster World

You don't need to move to the mountains. You don't need to delete every app. You don't need to quit your job, cancel your plans, or retreat from society.

You just need to choose different rhythms.

This might mean waking up without immediately checking your phone. It might mean driving in silence instead of playing another podcast. It might mean choosing one task and closing the rest. Saying no to things you once said yes to just because they were convenient, expected, or low-hanging fruit.

Slowing down is a discipline of subtraction.

Not because less is always better. But because less can finally become *enough*.

And in enough, you can hear yourself again.

You can hear the thoughts that matter, not just the ones that are loud. You can hear your own desires, not just the algorithm's. You can hear your conscience, which doesn't shout—it whispers.

The Stoics lived simply not to punish themselves, but to *see clearly*. Because simplicity is not aesthetic. It's awareness. It's the opposite of overstimulation. It's how you make space for what's essential to breathe.

And it's how you begin living your life—not just performing it.

VI. Becoming the Calm in the Room

You've probably met someone like this.

They walk in and don't rush to speak. They're grounded. You feel it. They don't match the tension in the room. They change it. They don't panic when others do. They listen longer. Speak slower. Move with something deeper than noise.

That's stillness in motion.

And it's not reserved for mystics or monks. It's available to you. But not by accident. Only through practice.

You practice by reclaiming small moments. You practice by pausing before reacting. By breathing before responding. By holding yourself with enough presence to ask, "Is this the energy I want to carry into this next moment?"

You won't get it right every time. You're human.

But the more you practice, the more people around you will feel it—even if you never say a word.

You'll become the calm in the room.

And eventually, that calm will no longer be something you do. It will be who you are.

That's the deepest form of discipline—not in what you achieve, but in how you carry yourself.

You become a steady flame in a world of wildfire.

And that steadiness spreads.

What Comes Next

You've arrived.

You've reclaimed your attention, rebuilt your values, fortified your inner world, refocused your energy, built structure, mastered emotion, and found your own rhythm in a noisy, chaotic time.

This is what discipline really is.

Not a set of rules. Not rigid routines. Not force or guilt or perfection.

But a way of being.

A quiet, powerful alignment between who you are and how you live.

Stillness doesn't mean nothing moves.

It means *you do not move unconsciously*.

It means you choose. You respond. You return.

And from that stillness, anything you build—any goal, any dream, any life—has a foundation that will not break.

But there's one final decision ahead.

And it will define everything that follows.

Let's talk about it in the conclusion.

Conclusion

Choose Your Chains: Distraction or Discipline

There is no such thing as freedom without discipline.

That truth might feel uncomfortable at first—especially in a world that sells you the idea that freedom means doing whatever you want, whenever you want, with no constraints and no cost. But if you've come this far, you've likely discovered something deeper. Something truer.

You've seen how easy it is to fall into a life of reactivity. How quickly your time, energy, and attention can be hijacked by the endless pull of distraction. You've felt how exhausting it is to chase clarity through chaos. And how quietly your sense of self erodes when every hour is spent in service of someone else's urgency.

But you've also seen the alternative.

You've seen what happens when you slow down. When you reclaim your time. When you wake up with intention and act with alignment. You've felt the quiet strength of doing one thing well, the relief of cutting the noise, the inner solidity of returning to your values—not once, but daily.

And now, at the end of this book, there's one more choice to make.

Not a complicated one. Not a dramatic one. Just a quiet, conscious decision that will echo through the rest of your life:

DISCIPLINE OVER DISTRACTION

Which chains will you wear?

Because one way or another, you will be bound to something.

You will be bound to distraction—the endless scrolling, the comparison loops, the pulled focus, the emotional whiplash, the shallow routines, the reactive days that blur into years. You'll be bound to noise. To urgency. To what the world wants from you before you've even asked what *you* want from yourself.

Or...

You will be bound to discipline.

To your values. Your code. Your chosen path. To rituals that center you. To focus that deepens you. To limits that liberate you. To small daily choices that don't always feel exciting but slowly, steadily, shape you into someone you trust.

Both paths require something from you. One takes it by force. The other offers it back to you in peace.

The Stoics believed that we are not free simply because we're untethered. We are free when we choose our constraints wisely—when we serve something higher than impulse, when we align with reason, when we live by a compass instead of a crowd.

You now have that compass.

It won't guarantee ease. But it *will* offer clarity. And in a time like ours, clarity is priceless.

So go forward—not as someone chasing perfection, but as someone returning to purpose.

You will get distracted. You will drift. But you will also remember.

And when you do, you'll come back—not to guilt, not to shame, but to structure. To stillness. To sovereignty.

To the life that is fully yours.

Because in the end, discipline isn't about control.

It's about *ownership*.

And you are ready now.

Keep the Discipline Alive

Now that you've walked the path through distraction toward discipline, stillness, and clarity, you carry with you more than knowledge—you carry *wisdom earned through reflection*. And that wisdom, like all good things, is meant to be shared.

If this book helped you reclaim your attention, build your inner fortress, or return to what truly matters, consider passing that strength on.

Leaving a review isn't just feedback. It's a form of service. It's a signal to others who are still lost in the noise—still seeking calm in a chaotic world—that they are not alone, and that a different way of living is possible.

Your words might be the nudge someone needs to pause. To reflect. To return to themselves.

Whether you bought this book on Amazon or elsewhere, your honest review can help fellow seekers discover these teachings—and find the calm, focus, and resilience they've been missing.

Thank you for walking this journey. And thank you, in advance, for helping others begin theirs.

If this book served you, we at Stoic School would be deeply grateful if you'd take a moment to leave a review.

Chapter-by-Chapter Summary

From Introduction – Why You're Not Broken

You're not lazy or broken—you're overwhelmed by a world designed to steal your attention. This book offers a return to intention through Stoic wisdom and personal discipline. It's not about fixing yourself, but about reclaiming your time, focus, and identity with clarity and calm.

From Chapter 1 – The War for Your Attention

Distraction isn't a personal flaw—it's a modern epidemic. This chapter exposes how your attention is constantly being hijacked, and shows how awareness, not willpower, is your first line of defense. Your life becomes what you focus on. The first step to freedom is noticing what's stealing your mind.

From Chapter 2 – The Stoic Code: Why Values Trump Willpower

Discipline that lasts is rooted in values, not fleeting motivation. Here, you build your personal Stoic code—clarity, courage, consistency—and shift from relying on effort to aligning with identity. When your actions reflect your values, discipline becomes natural, not forced.

From Chapter 3 – Building the Inner Citadel

Your inner citadel is your mental stronghold against chaos. This chapter helps you protect your mind from the noise of the world by strengthening awareness, setting boundaries, and creating space between stimulus and response. Stillness becomes your armor, and clarity your sword.

From Chapter 4 – The Rule of One: Mastering the Power of Single Focus

You don't need to do more—you need to focus on less. The Rule of One teaches you to simplify, subtract, and direct your full attention to what matters most. Depth beats speed. Clarity beats clutter. One clear focus can change everything.

From Chapter 5 – The Ritual Reset: Make Discipline Automatic

Discipline thrives on structure, not constant effort. Rituals—simple, intentional routines—help automate your values and anchor your day. This chapter shows you how to design a life that supports discipline by default, so you don't rely on willpower to stay aligned.

From Chapter 6 – Emotional Discipline: The Forgotten Superpower

Emotions are not the enemy—they're signals. This chapter teaches you to master anger, anxiety, shame, and envy without suppression. Through awareness and reflection, you gain control over how you respond, turning emotional storms into opportunities for self-command and growth.

From Chapter 7 – Stillness in Motion: Discipline in a Fast World

In a world obsessed with speed, real strength lies in slowing down. This chapter helps you find calm *within* action, moving with presence instead of panic. Stillness isn't still—it's intentional, steady, and rooted. You learn to remain centered, no matter the pace of life.

From Conclusion – Choose Your Chains: Distraction or Discipline

You'll serve something—either distraction or discipline. The final chapter calls you to consciously choose the path of self-ownership. Discipline isn't a cage; it's a commitment to your highest self. This is your invitation to live with clarity, calm, and the quiet strength of intention.

Free Bonus Reminder: 7-Day Challenge

In case you missed it at the start of the book, I've put together a **7-Day Overthinking Detox**, a simple, step-by-step plan to help you clear your mind, stop second-guessing, and make decisions with confidence. Each day, you'll get a quick, actionable challenge designed to rewire your brain and break the cycle of overthinking—without the overwhelm.

Scan the QR code below to grab your free copy and start the detox today.

References

Aurelius, M. (2002). *Meditations* (G. Hays, Trans.). Modern Library. (Original work published ca. 180)

Clear, J. (2018). *Atomic habits: An easy & proven way to build good habits & break bad ones*. Avery.

Duckworth, A. (2016). *Grit: The power of passion and perseverance*. Scribner.

Epictetus. (2008). *Discourses and selected writings* (R. Dobbin, Trans.). Penguin Classics.

Holiday, R. (2014). *The obstacle is the way: The timeless art of turning trials into triumph*. Portfolio.

Holiday, R., & Hanselman, S. (2016). *The daily stoic: 366 meditations on wisdom, perseverance, and the art of living*. Portfolio.

Kabat-Zinn, J. (2005). *Wherever you go, there you are: Mindfulness meditation in everyday life*. Hachette Books.

McKeown, G. (2014). *Essentialism: The disciplined pursuit of less*. Crown Business.

Newport, C. (2016). *Deep work: Rules for focused success in a distracted world*. Grand Central Publishing.

Ryan, R. M., & Deci, E. L. (2000). Self-determination theory and the facilitation of intrinsic motivation, social development, and well-being. *American Psychologist,* 55(1), 68–78. https://doi.org/10.1037/0003-066X.55.1.68

Seneca. (2004). *Letters from a Stoic* (R. Campbell, Trans.). Penguin Classics.

Seneca. (2010). *On the shortness of life* (C. D. N. Costa, Trans.). Penguin Books.

Don't miss out!

Visit the website below and you can sign up to receive emails whenever Stoic School publishes a new book. There's no charge and no obligation.

https://books2read.com/r/B-A-AWHQD-PGUEG

BOOKS 2 READ

Connecting independent readers to independent writers.

Also by Stoic School

Atomic Stillness: The Small Daily Disciplines of a Stoic Life
Master Calm Through Stoicism
Discipline Over Distraction
The Stoic Habit: Mastering Your Mind in a Chaotic World

www.ingramcontent.com/pod-product-compliance
Lightning Source LLC
LaVergne TN
LVHW090428210926
848480LV00002B/730
9798230985112